EX LIBRIS

KASHRUS HAKISHUF

S. Y. Zeitlin

Kashrus Hakishuf

Copyright © 2016 by S. Y. Zeitlin

ISBN 978-1-329-78631-8

KASHRUS HAKISHUF

The dedication of this book

Is split seven ways:

*To the **Ribono Shel Olam**;*

*To my **mother**, my **father**,*

*And both my **parents** (optimis parentibus);*

*To **M. P.**, who inspired me to write*

This book (you know whom you are);

*To **J. K. Rowling**, who single-handedly*

Revolutionized the world of children's

Literature (and asked for nothing in return

Except a few hundred million dollars);

*And to **Parry Otter**, the boy who lived.*

But not to you — I don't even know you.

Contents

KASHRUS HAKISHUF

KASHRUS HAKISHUF

Foreword

Much has been written about the Harry Potter series, and I am sure that even though the final installment was published over eight years ago, more will continue to be written. There is something about Harry Potter that captures and captivates, a feeling of timelessness and reality despite its obvious fantastical origins. If you don't believe me, just look at the facts. Harry Potter has become the best-selling book series in world history; it has sold more than 450 million copies worldwide and has been translated into six dozen languages, turning J. K. Rowling (for a time) into the world's first billionaire author. There is clearly something special about Harry Potter.

The aim of this work is to look at some of the many inconsistencies, discontinuities, and errors present in the Harry Potter series and discuss them in a Torahdige fashion. Please be aware that I am *not* one of those delusional authors who thinks Harry Potter and the Torah are actually based off of each other. I am simply presenting my personal opinions in a way consistent with Yiddishkeit with the goal of providing some Kosher reading material for those who are interested. Feel free to argue with anything posited herein.

KASHRUS HAKISHUF

The great author William Somerset Maugham is famous for stating, "There are three rules for writing a novel. Unfortunately, no one knows what they are." Luckily, this work is not a novel, so that shouldn't be an issue.

Seriously, though, I hope that you enjoy this work, and look forward to receiving your feedback.

S. Y. Zeitlin

syzeitlin@aol.com

January 2016

Queens, NY

KASHRUS HAKISHUF

Conventions Used in this Book

For the purposes of this book, the phrases "Harry Potter canon" and "Harry Potter series" are used to describe the ten books written by J. K. Rowling as well as comments made by J. K. Rowling on the internet or during interviews prior to the publication of the last book (*The Tales of Beedle the Bard*). This book may not necessarily pay credence to the eight movies produced by Warner Bros. or to information revealed by J. K. Rowling following the release of the last book.

In transliterating Hebrew and Yiddish words the prevalent Ashkenazic pronunciation has been used. All foreign terms have been capitalized to ease the reader's experience.

Whenever possible, quotes have been provided with sources. No guarantee is given as to the accuracy of these sources.

KASHRUS HAKISHUF

The following abbreviations have been used throughout this work:

JKR	J. K. Rowling
SS	*Harry Potter and the Sorcerer's Stone*
CS	*Harry Potter and the Chamber of Secrets*
PA	*Harry Potter and the Prisoner of Azkaban*
GF	*Harry Potter and the Goblet of Fire*
OP	*Harry Potter and the Order of the Phoenix*
HBP	*Harry Potter and the Half-Blood Prince*
DH	*Harry Potter and the Deathly Hallows*

PART ONE: HARRY POTTER: A SCRIPTURAL SYNOPSIS

KASHRUS HAKISHUF

Sefer B'reishis

In the *beginning* G-d created the Heaven and the Earth.
And also everything else. And Yiddin, and Goyim, and
Magic, to provide Nisyonos for the Yidden. Then world
history proceeded quite nicely until the thirty-first day of
July, 1980 L'fi Cheshbonam, when a little boy named
Harry was born to James and Lily Potter of Godric's
Hollow. Exactly one year and three months later, in the
three thousand, two hundred and ninety-second year after
Yetzias Mitzrayim, Kachatzos Halayla,[1] a Dark Wizard
named Voldemort murdered James and Lily. And he also
sought to kill Harry, but, B'hashgacha Pratis, his curse
rebounded, and Harry was spared. Then there was much
rejoicing throughout Wizarding Britain, and that day — 4
Cheshvan — was established as a Yom Mishteh V'simcha
L'dorei Doros.[2] And Great Britain *rested*.

And so Harry Potter grew up in the house of his
cousins, the Dursleys, which was quite unfortunate for him.
For they treated him as the unwanted orphan he was, and
they subjected him to cruel and unfair treatment for four
hundred years,[3] until G-d in his infinite mercy released him

---

PIRUSH RASHIZ

[1] Kachatzos Halayla. In fact, this occurred at exactly midnight; but the
term "Kachatzos" was used so that the astronomers would have no
room to doubt:

[2] Yom Mishteh V'simcha L'dorei Doros. To be celebrated as Purim
Edom:

[3] Four hundred years. In reality the letters began arriving after only ten
years, but those years were filled with such harsh torment that G-d
considered them as equivalent

9

from his torments. And it was that, shortly before his eleventh birthday, Harry Potter began to receive deluges of letters in the mail.[4] And these letters were continually suppressed by Uncle Vernon, until, on the eve of his eleventh birthday, Harry was rescued by a giant man who identified himself as Hagrid and explained that Harry was actually a Wizard and belonged in the Wizarding world, specifically Hogwarts School of Witchcraft and Wizardry. Then Hagrid took Harry to purchase his necessary school supplies from Diagon Alley. And he did so. Then Hagrid told Harry to *go for himself* from his land and the house of his uncle, to the platform[5] at King's Cross Station that he would show him.

Except that Hagrid didn't show him. But Harry *saw*, and he figured out how to reach the Hogwarts Express,[6] and befriended Ron Weasley in the process. *And the years*[7] of the life of the train were seven hours. Then Harry and his soon-to-be-schoolmates arrived at Hogwarts, where they learned about the history of its *generations*

PIRUSH RASHIZ

to four hundred. Davar Acheir, the four hundred years were counted beginning from the execution of Nearly Headless Nick (according to one Girsa):

[4] In the mail. Not, Chas V'shalom, by email, because that would be Assur Mid'oraisa. V'yesh Omrim because email was not yet in common usage. V'ha'ikar K'svara Rishonah:

[5] To the platform. This refers to Platform Nine and Three Quarters, the Gematria of "Uva," meaning "and he [Harry] should come":

[6] Hogwarts Express. Kishmo Kein Hu:

[7] And the years. This teaches us that the journey to Hogwarts was so long that it felt like years, V'hameivin Yavin:

10

before them, and were sorted into their Houses. And Harry was sorted into Gryffindor, *and he left* the Great Hall and went to the dormitories, were his luggage had been *sent, and he dwelled* there until *the end* of the year. And he learned the *approach* of magic, studying in many different classes, and became close friends with Ron Weasley and Hermione Granger. Together they had many adventures and occasionally got into trouble.[8] But Harry *lived* to survive the year, despite being confronted by the revivified Voldemort, whom Harry vanquished for a time. Gryffindor won the House Cup, then Harry went home for the summer.

Sefer Sh'mos

And these were the *names* of the friend whose letters Harry received over the summer.[9] And a house-elf named Dobby *appeared*, and he had suppressed Harry's letters, in the hopes that Harry would acquiesce to his demands not to return to Hogwarts. But Harry refused, and the Weasley boys rescued him from his imprisonment at the Dursleys, and took him to the Burrow, their home, where he *came*, and he *sent away* the warnings of Dobby. *Yet Ro*n dismissed Dobby as a rude practical joke that was probably against *the law*. Later they purchased their school supplies from Diagon Alley, where their soon-to-be professor, Gilderoy Lockhart, made a *donation* to Harry of his

---

PIRUSH RASHIZ

[8] Adventures… trouble. And sometimes both at the same time, such as when they defeated a raging Mountain Troll:

[9] Over the summer. No names are listed, for Harry did not actually receive any of the letters, K'dl'kaman:

11

complete set of books,[10] which the school list had *commanded* him to purchase.

Then upon attempting to enter Platform Nine and Three Quarters, Harry and Ron found the entrance to be blocked, and so they travelled to Hogwarts by *raising* themselves up in Arthur Weasley's flying car, but this got them into a great deal of trouble. And Dark Magic was at the work. For throughout that school year Harry heard a mysterious voice around the corridors, and students were attacked and petrified. This was at first thought to be the work of Hagrid and his former pet Acromantula, Aragog, so Hagrid was *assembled* and temporarily imprisoned. But it really *amounted* to the plot of the memory of Tom Riddle[11] and Slytherin's Basilisk hidden in the elusive Chamber of Secrets. And Harry defeated Riddle, saving Hogwarts from closure.

Sefer Vayikra I

And it was around Harry's thirteenth birthday that the mad Wizard Sirius Black, a notorious mass murderer, escaped from Azkaban Prison. And Harry angrily blew up his Aunt Marge, so he ran away from the Dursleys, *and he called* out for help, and the Knight Bus transported him to the Leaky Cauldron, where he was greeted by the Minister of Magic,

---

PIRUSH RASHIZ
[10] Set of books. These included *Break with a Banshee, Gadding with Ghouls, Holidays with Hags, Magical Me, Marauding with Monsters, The Travel Trilogy, Travels with Trolls, Voyages with Vampires, Wanderings with Werewolves,* and *Year with the Yeti:*
[11] Tom Riddle. This was Voldemort as a student:

KASHRUS HAKISHUF

Cornelius Fudge, and met Ron and Hermione, and spent the remainder of the summer holiday. And they travelled on the Hogwarts Express, but they were accosted by a Dementor, and Harry passed out and recalled memories of the night his parents were killed, but Professor Remus Lupin, who was in their compartment, *commanded* the Dementor to leave,[12] and as he commanded, so it did. And the Dementors cast a Dark pall over Hogwarts as well as all of Wizarding Britain, especially affecting Harry. Later, in Hogsmeade, Harry overheard that Sirius Black had been the one who betrayed his parents to Voldemort, and knew[13] that Black sought now to kill Harry himself. And Harry was not afraid, as[14] he was enraged.

And around *the eighth day* of the month of January Harry began receiving Patronus Charm lessons from Professor Lupin, for Harry said, lest a Dementor attacking me unawares, leaving me defenseless. And Harry became proficient. His Patronus took the form of a stag. And school continued. Until Ron, Harry, and Hermione were lured into the Shrieking Shack by a black dog, which turned out to be Sirius Black, who was an Animagus. But it was that Sirius was neither insane nor evil, for in truth it

---

PIRUSH RASHIZ

[12] To leave. Lupin did this by use of the Patronus Spell. V'ayin L'kaman:

[13] Knew. How did he now know this? Rather, he knew it earlier, for he had overheard Arthur Weasley warning his wife about it:

[14] As. This means "rather," as we have learned: "As" may be used to mean four terms: if, perhaps, rather, because:

had been Peter Pettigrew[15] who had betrayed Harry's parents, and Pettigrew was also an Animagus, and he was Ron's rat. But then Professor Lupin, who had discovered them, turned into a wolf, for he was a werewolf. And Pettigrew escaped, and Sirius was captured, for the world did not know that he was not evil, and he was subjected to the Dementor's Kiss. But Dumbledore, the brilliant Headmaster of Hogwarts, realized the truth, and he instructed Hermione and Harry to go back in time[16] to save Sirius and Buckbeak.[17] And as Dumbledore said, so they did, and they rescued Sirius, and he fled to safety on Buckbeak, and went into hiding. But a small seed of hope was *borne* in Harry, for Sirius was his godfather, and now Harry had family.

Sefer Vayikra II

At the end of that summer holiday Harry was invited by the Weasleys to join them and Hermine at the final of the four hundred and twenty-second Quidditch World Cup. There there were wizards from all over the world, for they had come to see Ireland play Bulgaria and support their teams. The match began with the team's respective mascots,

---

PIRUSH RASHIZ

[15] Peter Pettigrew. He was one of James Potter's school friends, along with Remus Lupin and Sirius Black. From here they said the expression, "Save me, today, from an evil friend":

[16] Back in time. For Hermione had a Time-Turner, which she used to attend more classes then otherwise possible:

[17] Buckbeak. He was Hagrid's hippogriff, which had been sentenced to death after Draco Malfoy, a Slytherin student, claimed it violently attacked him:

*lepre*chauns and Veela, and Ireland won the Cup.[18] But the festivities were interrupted by the appearance of Death Eaters, and the Dark Mark, a sign that had been used by Voldemort *after the death* of a victim, was cast.

Then they arrived at Hogwarts, and Dumbledore announced that Hogwarts would be hosting the Triwizard Tournament along with two other schools, Durmstrang and Beauxbatons. The new DADA[19] teacher was the battle-worn, *holey*[20] Professor Alastor Moody, and he taught them the Unforgivable Curses. And the Goblet of Fire that was used to designate contestants for the Triwizard Tournament selected Durmstrang's Victor Krum, and Beauxbatons' Fleur Delacour, and Hogwarts' Cedric Diggory, and then also Harry, even though he was too young, for someone had used Dark magic to confuse the Goblet, but Harry had no choice but to compete. But his friends did not believe Harry's claims that he had not been the one to do so, although he *said* that he had not been the one to do so. And over the year in addition to schoolwork there were tasks. And the tasks included stealing an egg from a dragon, and recuing a captured friend hidden in the Lake, and locating the Triwizard Cup hidden inside a gigantic hedge maze as big as a *mountain*. But the last task was a trap, for Harry found the Cup, but he was transported to a graveyard,

---

PIRUSH RASHIZ

[18] Ireland won the Cup. V'af Al Pi Kein, Bulgaria's Seeker, Viktor Krum, caught the Snitch:

[19] DADA. Roshei Teivos for Defense Against the Dark Arts:

[20] Holey. This teaches us that he was missing an eye, a leg, and a chunk of his nose:

15

where Diggory was murdered and Peter Pettigrew brought
Voldemort back to life, and Voldemort sought *in his ways*
to kill Harry. But Harry managed to escape, and
Voldemort went into hiding. And Harry explained what
had occurred to Dumbledore, and they realized that
Professor Moody was actually Death Eater Barty Crouch,
Jr., disguised by the Polyjuice Potion. But the world did
not believe Harry that Voldemort had returned, for they did
not want to.

Sefer Bamidbar I

And Harry spoke to his cousin, Dudley, *in a deserted*
alleyway, warning him of the impending danger. For they
were, impossibly, attacked by Dementors, forcing Harry to
use *raise* his wand and cast the Patronus Charm. And
Harry was nearly expelled from Hogwarts, but Dumbledore
intervened, and he was sentenced to a disciplinary hearing
at the Ministry, which he passed, with G-d's mercy, and
returned to Hogwarts after staying at Number Twelve
Grimmauld Place, the home of Sirius Black and new
headquarters of the Order of the Phoenix, Dumbledore's
organization in opposition of Voldemort.

But Hogwarts had changed, for there was a new
DADA[21] professor, Dolores Umbridge, who was sent by
the Ministry to control Hogwarts; and she was evil, and she
denied Voldemort's return, and she severely punished
Harry for refusing to do so. And when Harry *ascended* to

PIRUSH RASHIZ
[21] DADA. Ayin L'eil:

the Owlery to *send* a letter to Sirius Black, he discovered that Umbridge was cunningly searching select students' mail. And she also refused to teach actual defense magic, instead teaching worthless information from Ministry-approved books. And this angered Harry and his classmates to the *core*, so Hermione and Ron persuaded[22] Harry to form and lead a student organization[23] in which they would actually learn DADA. And Harry did so, and many students joined, including Anthony Goldstein.

But Harry began having visions of Voldemort, including one in which Nagini[24] attacked Arthur Weasley, so Dumbledore arranged for Harry to take Occlumency lessons with Professor Severus Snape, but they did not help, for there was much hatred between Harry and Snape, because of his father.[25] Then Umbridge found out about Dumbledore's Army, and she got the Ministry involved, and Dumbledore was forced to flee Hogwarts, and Umbridge took over as Headmistress, and she made many *laws*[26] that were unfair and cruel, and it was a Dark time for

---

PIRUSH RASHIZ

[22] Persuaded. This teaches us that Harry was at first reluctant, and only after much convincing did he acquiesce:

[23] Organization. And they called this group Dumbledore's Army, as it is written below:

[24] Nagini. This was Voldemort's snake, called so Al Shem her large appearance and evilness, as it was said, "K'sheholeich L'medinas Hayam, Kor'im L'nachash 'Nagini'":

[25] His father. For Snape was a student together with James Potter, and they were bitter enemies, and Snape resented him:

Hogwarts. Fred and George Weasley attempted to lighten the mood by organizing large-scale pranks on Hogwarts and Umbridge, and they eventually left Hogwarts and fulfilled their dream of establishing a joke shop in Diagon Alley. As the year ended, Harry and his classmates took their O.W.L.s.[27] But Harry had a vision, and he saw his godfather, Sirius Black, held captive in the Ministry of Magic's Department of Mysteries about which he had been dreaming, so he flew[28] there together with fellow students Ron, Hermione, Ginny Weasley, Neville Longbottom, and Luna Lovegood, expecting to do battle with Voldemort. But it was a trap, for Voldemort had planted a false vision in Harry's mind, for he wanted Harry to retrieve form the Department of Mysteries a prophecy concerning Harry's magical relationship with him. And the Order of the Phoenix came to aid them, and Sirius Black was killed. Then Voldemort himself appeared, but Dumbledore came and forced him to flee, but not before the Cornelius Fudge and Ministry members saw him. And the world was forced to acknowledge that Voldemort had returned,[29] and many Death Eaters were imprisoned in Azkaban. But the prophecy had been destroyed. Yet Dumbledore revealed its

---

PIRUSH RASHIZ

[26] Unfair laws. And this is what they called Educational Decrees:

[27] O.W.L.s. Roshei Teivos for Ordinary Wizarding Exams, "Regents" B'la'az.

[28] Flew there. But how did he fly there? Was not his broomstick confiscated by Professor Umbridge? Rather, they flew there on the backs of thestrals:

[29] Returned. And Cornelius Fudge, who had for so long denied the truth of Harry's words, was fired, K'derech Rov politicians:

contents to Harry, for it stated that ultimately, Harry and Voldemort would battle to the death.

Sefer Bamidbar II

And Harry left the Dursleys' house for the penultimate time, guided by Dumbledore, who took him to convince[30] an old potions teacher, Horace Slughorn, to return to Hogwarts, then to the Weasleys, where he *wasted* away his time stayed until the beginning of school with Ron and Hermione. There they received their O.W.L. grades.

That year Harry received private lessons from Dumbledore regarding Voldemort and how to defeat him, and Dumbledore told him about Horcruxes,[31] which Voldemort used to become immortal. One such object was the ancient locket of Salazar Slytherin, which was similar to the *mouth of a serpent*. And again Dark forces were at work, for assassination attempts were made that ended up severely injuring students Katie Bell and Ron. Harry suspected Draco Malfoy, and he was correct. For when Dumbledore invited Harry to join him in attempting to locate a Horcrux, Draco secretly admitted Death Eaters into Hogwarts, and they did battle there. And when Dumbledore returned, Draco had been ordered by Voldemort to kill him. But Draco was unable to do so, and

---

PIRUSH RASHIZ

[30] Convince. Ayin L'eil B'he'arah 22:

[31] Horcruxes. This was a method Voldemort used to split his soul into seven part, which he hid in magically significant objects, as Dumbledore found out by viewing a memory which he instructed Harry to acquire from Professor Slughorn:

KASHRUS HAKISHUF

Severus Snape, whom Dumbledore and his *staff* had for so long trusted, murdered Dumbledore in hid stead. And Harry was enraged, but Snape and the Death Eaters exultantly escaped, *travelling* to Voldemort. And all of Hogwarts grieved for Dumbledore, and they buried him there.[32]

Sefer Devarim

And these are the *things* that occurred to Harry as he left the Dursleys for the final time. And the Dursleys *pled* to remain in their home, but the Wizards warned them it would no longer be safe. So they left. Then the Order of the Phoenix came, and they planned to help Harry escape to the Weasleys without being apprehended by the Death Eaters. So seven of them used Polyjuice Potion to transform into the visage of Harry, the hopes that this ruse would confuse their foes. But this plan went wrong, *when* Voldemort himself appeared, and Harry was nearly captured. And many were injured, and Alastor Moody was killed. And the survivors *saw*, and they grieved. But life went on, and Bill Weasley married Fleur Delacour. But even as they celebrated, the Ministry fell to the Death Eaters. And Harry, Ron, and Hermione, who had *judged* and prepared for such an emergency, *went* into hiding. And they *came* to Grimmauld Place, and befriended Kreacher,

---

PIRUSH RASHIZ

[32] There. On the outskirts of Hogwarts Castle, as per Dumbledore's wishes, as we have learned, Mitzva L'kayeim Divrei Hameis:

20

the house-elf whom Sirius had hated, and he led them to the real locket[33] of Slytherin.

But in retrieving the locket from the Ministry, for it *stood* there in the possession of Dolores Umbridge, they accidentally revealed[34] Grimmauld Place to the Death Eater Yaxley, so they were force to hide in the forests. And Ron grew restless and left for a period, but he repented and returned. Before that Harry and Hermione travelled to Godric's Hollow to visit Harry's birthplace, but there there was a trap, and they narrowly avoided being captured by Voldemort. Then *they went* to the home of Xenophilius Lovegood, Luna's father, and he told them about the Deathly Hallows, a trio of legendary magical objects said to grant their owner immortality. And Harry was convinced that the legend was true, much to the consternation of Hermione, for they were meant to be concentrating on locating the Horcruxes. Then they were captured and sent to Malfoy Manor,[35] and Hermione was tortured, but with the aid of Dobby they escaped to Shell Cottage,[36] the home of Bill and Fleur. And they disguised themselves and entered Gringotts Bank, and retrieved a Horcrux that was hidden there, and escaped on the back of a dragon. Then

---

PIRUSH RASHIZ

[33] Real locket. For the locket discovered by Dumbledore prior to his death had actually been a fake, designed to deceive Voldemort:

[34] Revealed. V'yeish Kamah Midrashim Al Zeh, Aval L'pshuto Shel Mikra Ani Ba L'fareish:

[35] Malfoy Manor. K'shmo Kein Hu:

[36] Shell Cottage. V'yeish Kamah Midrashim Al Zeh, Aval L'pshuto Shel Mikra Ani Ba L'fareish:

they proceeded to Hogwarts, and joined hidden students who were loyal to them and *listened* to Harry; and they located the remaining Horcruxes and destroyed them. But much innocent[37] blood was shed. Then Voldemort murdered Severus Snape for his own purpose, and Harry found out that Snape had really been innocent[38] and acting on Dumbledore's bidding. Then Harry surrendered himself to Voldemort, and Voldemort killed him. And Harry awoke and saw a vision of Dumbledore, who told him the truth about the Horcruxes and the Deathly Hallows, and *blessed* Harry. And Harry lived. And he once again fought Voldemort, and he killed Voldemort, and he was the Boy Who Lived. And Harry and his friends grew up and married and had children and lived their lives. And all was well.

PIRUSH RASHIZ

[37] Much innocent. "Much" is not coming but to exclude, and what does it teach us? That some guilty parties were also killed, and this refers to many Death Eaters:

[38] Innocent. From here they said, "Dan Es Kol Ha'adam L'kaf Zechus":

Tam V'nishlam:

PART TWO: INYANIM SHONIM

KASHRUS HAKISHUF

A Yid in Hogwarts

Source

"I had the idea — that it might be good if people who wanted to study Defense Against the Dark Arts — and I mean, really study it, you know, not the rubbish that Umbridge is doing with us because nobody could call that Defense Against the Dark Arts—"

—Hermione Granger

"Hear, hear."

—Anthony Goldstein, OP

Introduction

Anthony Goldstein is a blond-haired, blue-eyed wizard in the same year as Harry Potter. He is sorted into Ravenclaw and joins Padma Patil as a prefect in OP. On December 16, 2014 — a day that will live in infamy — JKR, in response to a reader's query, posted on Twitter: "Anthony Goldstein, Ravenclaw, Jewish wizard." This has led to much speculation and numerous fanfictions, foremost of which is Laazov's *Goldstein* at fanfiction.net (which we strongly encourage everyone to read; much of this chapter was inspired by it).

KASHRUS HAKISHUF

A Closer Look

Frumkeit

The most obvious way to get out of all the complex
Halachic issues posed to a Jewish student at Hogwarts is to
note that there is no reason to assume that Anthony
Goldstein is Frum. However, this takes all the fun out of
everything, and is therefore an imprudent Pshat.
ANTHONY IS FRUM. Got it? Good.

Kashrus Hakishuf

The first and most important issue to be dealt with is the
numerous Issurei D'oraisa connected with performing
magic, primarily "M'chasheifah Lo Sichayeh."
(Incidentally, the Rambam in Hilchos Avodas Kochavim
lists no less than eleven Issurim in relation to performing
witchcraft.)

There is a well-known Machlokes regarding these
Issurim. The aforementioned Rambam holds that true
sorcery does not and has never existed; those who claim to
practice magic are merely charlatans. The Ramban and
Ran, however, posit that magical powers do exist, and it is
this which the Torah forbids. Evidently, JKR Paskens like
the latter view. This is in line with the Gra, who famously
states that the Rambam's Shitah was influenced by the
"philosophers" and has no Halachic basis.

The relevant Nafkah Minah would be if it is
permissible to utilize magic in a case of Sakanas Nefashos:
According to the Rambam, since sorcery is in any case
meaningless, it will always be forbidden to make use of

apparent magic. According to the other Rishonim, on the other hand, we would apply the Din of "V'chai Bahem" to permit magic by a Sakanas Nefashos.

The Maharshal and the Mishkenos Yaakov both Pasken L'halacha that, in a case of Sakanas Nefashos, it would indeed be permissible to make use of sorcery (contingent upon the assumption that doing so will not constitute Avodah Zarah).

Now we must determine if refraining from attending Hogwarts is indeed a case of Sakanas Nefashos. It is clear from the series that underage (i.e., accidental) magic is not a rarity; magical children who have not yet learned to control their abilities are prone to causing dangerous and potentially deadly incidents. Just a few examples of this include Harry releasing a boa constrictor from its exhibit at the zoo; Harry inflating his Aunt Marge; young Snape causing a tree branch to hit Petunia Evans; and, fatally, Ariana Dumbledore exploding her mother. It is thus evident that it would be Sakanas Nefashos not to learn how to control one's magic.

It is therefore permissible — in fact, Halachically obligatory — for a Jewish wizard to attend a wizarding school such as Hogwarts to learn how to control his powers. In the remaining sections, we will discuss how Anthony could overcome the challenges presented by being a Yid in the Hogwarts environment.

KASHRUS HAKISHUF

The first issue that comes to mind is how to keep Kashrus. (Let's assume that Anthony would not want to subsist solely on fruits and vegetables for an entire year.) Hermione lets us know in DH that food is the first of the five Principal Exceptions to Gamp's Law of Elemental Transfiguration. Thus, all food served at the Hogwarts Great Hall must have been cooked in the castle's kitchen by house-elves.

There does not seem to be any reason why the house-elves could not order shipments of Kosher ingredients and prepare them in a manner compliant with Hilchos Kashrus. Anthony himself can serve as a Mashgiach. For more information, see *Kitzur Shulchan Aruch* 38:2.

The other concern posed by house-elves preparing food is Bishul Akum. A complete discussion of these Halachos is beyond the scope of this work. For Anthony's purposes, it is sufficient to know that Rav Moshe (*Igros Moshe* Y.D. 45) brings down that the Gezeirah of Bishul Akum was only made for cases in which intermarriage might occur as a result. Since it is reasonable to assume that house-elves do not intermarry with Goyim, we can conclude that the Issur does not apply to them. Keep in mind that this is contingent upon the fact that Bishul Akum is a Din forbidding food cooked by a Goy per se, as opposed to a requirement for food to be cooked by a Yid. While house-elves are certainly not Yidden, it is

28

understandable that they would not fall into the Geder of Ovdei Kochavim, either.

Minyan

As a Frum Yid, Anthony is required to Daven with a Minyan three times a day. Yet Hogwarts students are, with rare exceptions, prohibited from leaving the castle grounds over the course of the school year. It is possible that Anthony could receive a special dispensation to travel to Shul for Davening, either by Floo powder, portkey, or side-along apparition. However, this would greatly interfere with his class schedule, as well as pose a safety concern. In addition, the Hogwarts administration would likely be hesitant to allow Anthony to mingle with Muggles on a daily basis, as doing so could lead to a breach of the International Statute of Secrecy. Finding himself in such a situation, is Anthony still obligated to Daven with a Minyan?

The *Mishnah Berurah* (90) Paskens that one is only obligated to travel up to a distance of one Mil from his residence (or four Mil if he is travelling) in order to Daven with a Minyan. One Mil is equivalent to slightly more than half a mile, or an eighteen-minute walk. The modern-day Poskim discuss whether nowadays, when travelling by car is prevalent, one would be required to drive for this amount of time in order to reach a minyan. In Anthony's situation, since it would be extremely difficult to regularly Daven with a Minyan, L'chorah he can rely on the Poskim who hold that he is considered an Oneis and thus Patur from Tefillah B'tzibbur.

KASHRUS HAKISHUF

Shabbos and Yom Tov

The final challenge that Anthony will have to take care of is observance of Shabbos and Yomim Tovim. As we will discuss later, it is clear that Hogwarts makes exceptions for religious students. Shabbos would not pose a problem in any event, as Hogwarts does not hold classes over the weekend, beginning from Friday afternoon. For the longer Yomim Tovim, Anthony will obviously have to make up the work that he missed, but it should be simple enough to receive permission to absent himself from classes.

KASHRUS HAKISHUF

Hogwarts and Religion

Source

Hogwarts is a multifaith school.

—J. K. Rowling, October 16, 2007 interview

Introduction

JKR has stated numerous times that she specifically avoided using the series as a vehicle to promote religion. In fact, she notably refused to speak about canonical religion at all until after the release of DH, and even then she was quite careful about what she said. (This, unfortunately, did not put an end to the scores of often violent religious debates over the series.)

In any event, assuming that Hogwarts is by and large a nonreligious organization, from a purely statistical point of view there will always be some students who come from religious backgrounds.

A Closer Look

According to the United Kingdom's 2001 census, which was taken (by most calculations) just a few years after the events of DH, approximately 45,150,000 people, or 76% of the population, affiliated themselves with a particular religion. Of these, 70% were Christian, 3% Muslim, and 0.45% Jewish. This numbers can be used to determine, statistically, the average number of religious students who attended Hogwarts during this period.

KASHRUS HAKISHUF

Exactly how many students attend Hogwarts during the series is a matter of well-known controversy. JKR has stated at interviews that she imagined this number to be one thousand. However, simple mathematical calculations based on the series place the amount at no more than three hundred, so we'll stick with this conservative estimate. A great majority of Christian students would probably not, in reality, practice much religion; but this would not be the case for other religions. Proportionally, using the above figures, it can be computed that Hogwarts houses a grand total of one Jewish student per population. In other words, Hogwarts accepts one new Yid every seven-year cycle. Perfect! That one student is Anthony Goldstein.

In addition to Anthony, as we have mentioned, there are surely several other devout religious students at Hogwarts. It is safe to assume, then, that the administration of Hogwarts would be unhesitant to make allowances for them, in terms of regular practices, habits, and holidays. This makes life for Anthony (and us!) quite a bit easier.

KASHRUS HAKISHUF

The Deathly Hallows: Magic Mid'oraisa

Source

> "The Elder Wand," he said, and he drew a straight vertical line on the parchment. "The Resurrection Stone," he said, and he added a circle on top of the line. "The Cloak of Invisibility," he finished, enclosing both line and circle in a triangle, to make the symbol that so intrigued Hermione. "Together," he said, "the Deathly Hallows."
>
> —Xenophilius Lovegood, DH

Introduction

The Deathly Hallows are three highly powerful magical objects allegedly created by Death and granted to the three Peverell brothers. The Hallows are comprised of the Elder Wand, an extremely powerful and supposedly unbeatable wand; the Resurrection Stone, a stone with the ability to communicate with the spirits of the dead; and the Cloak of Invisibility, which renders its wearer completely invisible. According to legend, Ignotus, the youngest and wisest brother, utilized the cloak to successfully escape from Death. It is believed that one who possess all three Hallows will become the invincible "Vanquisher of Death."

A Closer Look

It has been suggested that the Deathly Hallows find their Mekor in none other than Parshas Vayeishev. Regarding the Ma'aseh Yehudah V'tamar, the Torah states that Tamar demanded from Yehudah a Mashkon consisting of "Chosamcha Ufsilecha Umatcha Asher B'yadecha," "Your *signet*, your *cloak*, and the *stick* which is in your hand." Sound slightly familiar? Even more enlightening is the Gemara (Ta'anis 5b) which states, "Ya'akov Avinu Lo Meis" — "Ya'akov Avinu never died." The Torah never explains what ended up happening with Yehudah's ring, cloak, and stick... is it possible that his father, Ya'akov, got ahold of them? (Please be aware that we are NOT, Chas V'Sholom, claiming that the Torah actually contains an allusion to the Deathly Hallows; nor are deluded enough to believe that JKR consulted the Chumash before writing DH. Still, it seem like a mighty strange coincidence....)

KASHRUS HAKISHUF

Shichrur of House-Elves

Source

"You know, house-elves get a very raw deal! It's slavery, that's what it is...Why doesn't anyone do something about it?"

—Hermione, GB

"A house-elf must be set free, sir."

—Dobby, CH

Introduction

House-elves are small, humanoid, magical creatures that are typically employed by old, wealthy Wizarding families. They are bound to serve their masters until dying or receiving freedom by being presented with clothing. Despite their usually cruel and brutal treatment, house-elves are extremely obsequious and consider it a matter of pride that they faithfully serve their families. Hogwarts employs over one hundred house-elves for custodial and kitchen services.

A Closer Look

Throughout the series, numerous mention is made to the Shichrur or attempted liberating of house-elves. As Dobby informs Harry Potter at the beginning of CS, a house-elf can only be freed if his Adon presents him with clothes. However, how this is accomplished gets a bit complicated. Let's go through some of the issues step by step.

KASHRUS HAKISHUF

At the conclusion of CS, Harry tricks Lucius Malfoy intro feeing Dobby by throwing him one of Harry's socks. It appears from here that (a) a house-elf can be freed Ba'al Korcho of the Adon; and (b) the garment used to free said house-elf does not need to be owned by the Adon, as long as it Birshus Ha'adon immediately prior to the house-elf receiving it. Additionally, from Barty Coruch, Sr. freeing Winky in GF as a gesture of his disappointment, we see that (c) a house-elf can be freed Ba'al Korcho (against his own will).

Now's where things start getting tricky. One of the plot points of OP is S.P.E.W., Hermione Granger's makeshift organization dedicated to ensuring the liberty of house-elves, particularly in Hogwarts. Hermione attempts to free unsuspecting house-elves by hiding hand-knitted hats around the common room in areas where house-elves will unintentionally pick them up. It is natural to assume that Hermione, one of the brightest witches of her time, is familiar with the laws of Shichrur of house-elves. And, in fact, the house-elves cease cleaning the Gryffindor common room for fear of being up Hermione's hats. Evidently, if a house-elf were to pick up such a hat, his freedom would ensue.

But what, exactly, were the house-elves so afraid of? Granted that house-elves can be freed against their will, and even against the will of the Adon, surely some sort of action on the part of the Adon is required. Yet Hermione does not own the Hogwarts house-elves — they belong to the castle itself (and perhaps, by extension, to the

36

KASHRUS HAKISHUF

Headmaster and Board of Governors)! And even if it was the case that every Hogwarts student is granted a partial ownership of its house-elves, that should only enable a given student to renounce her ownership of her specific portion of each house-elf — at most, affording them a status of Chatzi Eved Chatzi Ben Chorin. What was Hermione thinking?

B'docheik, we can answer that Hermione really knew that her plan was full of flaws, but she went through with it anyway, just to give it a chance. Hermione's plan backfired on her, however. Instead of accepting her hats, the house-elves were so insulted that they refused to continue cleaning the Gryffindor common room, leaving Dobby to do all the work… and get all of the hats.

KASHRUS HAKISHUF

The Fidelius Charm: Gavrah or Cheftzah?

Source

> "An immensely complex spell involving the magical concealment of a secret inside a single, living soul. The information is hidden inside the chosen person, or Secret-Keeper, and is henceforth impossible to find — unless, of course, the Secret-Keeper chooses to divulge it."
>
> — Filius Flitwick, PA

Introduction

One of the most difficult anomalies present in the canon is the Fidelius Charm, an ancient spell used to protect those in danger by magically hiding their place of residence from foes. The location is concealed inside the soul of the Secret-Keeper, rendering it invisible and intangible to everyone else, except for those to whom the Secret-Keeper chooses to divulge. It is notably used by James and Lily Potter to protect their home in Godric's Hollow and Albus Dumbledore for the Order of the Phoenix's headquarters at Grimmauld Place, as well as by Arthur and Bill Weasley on their respective households. However, over the course of the series, a number of discrepancies develop as to the exact nature of the Fidelius Charm.

A Closer Look

Although are unaware of the fact at the time, the first time we encounter the Fidelius Charm is in the very first chapter of the series, when Hagrid tells Dumbledore that he personally rescued baby Harry from the ruins of the Potter home. Evidently, the Fidelius Charm placed there had ceased to be in effect, or Hagrid would not have been able to see Harry. But why would the deaths of Lily and James end the Fidelius Charm? We know from PA that the Potters' Secret-Keeper was Peter Pettigrew; as far as we know, Pettigrew never had reason to reveal the secret to Hagrid. (Incidentally, why on earth would the Potters make Peter Pettigrew their Secret-Keeper? Why not a much more powerful, secure wizard such a Dumbledore — or, for that matter, themselves?)

It is possible, but very unlikely, that once the house was ruined, the charm ceased to exist, because the secret was no longer true — the Potters weren't hiding in that specific house anymore, as it had just been destroyed. But it makes much more sense to explain that although the Potters were not the Secret-Keepers, one of them was the caster of the Fidelius Charm; when the charm's caster dies, its protection does end, and the secret becomes revealed.

Fast forward a few years. At the beginning of OP, Harry is led by members of the Order to its new headquarters, Number Twelve Grimmauld Place. Alastor Moody shows Harry a piece a parchment upon which Dumbledore — the Order's Secret-Keeper — has written this address; only then can Harry see the house. As Sirius Black explains to Harry, "Dumbledore's Secret-Keeper for the Order, you know — nobody can find Headquarters unless he tells them personally where it is." Apparently, a

KASHRUS HAKISHUF

Fidelius secret can only be revealed in person or in writing by the original Secret-Keeper, and those to whom the secret is revealed are unable to tell it to anyone else (otherwise, Moody could simply have told Harry about Headquarters himself).

Fast forward again. In DH, Arthur Weasley explains that following the death of Dumbledore, each of the people to whom Dumbledore had confided Grimmauld Place's location had become a Secret-Keeper in turn. As a result of this, the Order is forced to move the location of its headquarters to the Burrow. Note that the concern is not that the secret had become publicly revealed, just that there were now twenty times as many Secret-Keepers, diluting the power of the charm.

In the aftermath of their adventurous escapade from the Ministry of Magic, Hermione explains to Harry and Ron why it is no longer safe to stay at Grimmauld Place: "As we Disapparated, Yaxley caught hold of me... we arrived at Grimmauld Place... I've already taken him inside the Fidelius Charm's protection. Since Dumbledore died, we're Secret-Keepers, so I've given him the secret, haven't I?" Hold on one second. Even though Hermione is a Secret-Keeper, how did carrying Yaxley to Grimmauld Place reveal the secret to him? Nothing was explained to him; Hermione did not tell or write to Yaxley about the location. And even if, for some heretofore unmentioned reason, merely showing a protected location to an outsider reveals its secret to him, why couldn't Hermione simply stun Yaxley and throw him out of the house? As we proved above, even someone who is told a Secret by its Keeper does not have the ability to reveal it to others, so Yaxley would not have been able to let his fellow Death Eaters know about it!

One final example: Imprisoned in Malfoy Manor, Harry engineers an escape plan involving Dobby the house-elf. Harry tells Dobby to take Dean Thomas, Luna Lovegood, and Ollivander and Apparate to Shell Cottage, the residence of Bill and Fleur Weasley. Dobby manages to locate Shell cottage and bring all of them there safety, then following suit with Harry, Ron, and Hermione. But, as Bill later informs Harry, Shell Cottage is protected by the Fidelius Charm. How could Dobby, then, enter — or even notice — the house? Even if house-elves' magical abilities allow them to bypass the Fidelius Charm (which would be a huge security flaw), surely that would not extend to Dean, Luna, Ollivander, Harry, Ron, and Hermione. The only possibility is that the Fidelius Charm was added to Shell Cottage sometime after they had all arrived. But if this is the case, how is Harry able to re-enter the newly-protected Shell Cottage after leaving it to bury Dobby?

To explain this perplexity, perhaps we can Klar a Chakirah: Is the protection of the Fidelius Charm a Din in the Gavrah (that is, in the people from whom the secret is hidden) or in the Cheftzah (that is, in the secret information itself)? If it is a Din in the Cheftzah, then its protection is unassailable; once the location becomes a secret, even someone who is standing right outside would magically forget about it. However, if it is really a Din in the Gavrah, we can answer that someone who is in sight of the location during the charm's casting is impervious to its effects. Thus Harry, who was just at the outskirts of Shell Cottage as Bill was performing the Fidelius Charm, did not need to be let in on the secret.

So, as a Sikkum, it emerges L'maskanah that: when a Secret-Keeper dies, the secret dies with him, and anyone else who knows the secret becomes a Secret-Keeper; only people who were personally informed of the secret before his death or were within the premises of the location at the time of the charm's casting can know the secret; and when the charm's caster dies, the charm ceases to protect, that is, the secret becomes revealed to all. It still remains unclear why Hermione was so concerned about Yaxley being shown Grimmauld Place. V'tzarich Iyun.

PART THREE: PLOTHOLES: PIRUSHIM AND P'SHATIM

KASHRUS HAKISHUF

Sorcerer's Stone

I. In Chapter Two, the boa constrictor at the zoo winks at Harry. This is impossible, as snakes do not have eyelids; instead, their eyes are protected by transparent scales.

    a. Maybe Harry just imagined the snake winking at him.

    b. Perhaps being in the vicinity of Parselmouths imbues snakes with certain otherwise impossible abilities.

II. Furthermore, why does the boa constrictor wink at Harry? How does it know that Harry is a Parselmouth in the first place?

    a. Assuming that Harry really just imagined the snake winking at him, this is not a Kasha.

    b. Ein Hachah Nami; snakes are indeed cognizant of Parselmouths and can communicate without prior initiation.

III. In Chapter Five, Hagrid and Harry use the Dursleys' boat to get back to shore. So how do the Dursleys get back home?

    a. Eventually, the owner of the boat (the "toothless old man") must have wanted it back, and used another boat to sail to the "Hut-on-the-Rock," where he was no doubt quite surprised to find three Dursleys but no boat.

IV.   In Chapter Five, Hagrid tells Harry, "There's not a single witch or wizard who went bad who wasn't in Slytherin." What about Sirius Black — he was in Gryffindor, and at this point in time the entire Wizarding world thinks that he is a mass murderer who betrayed Lily and James Potter to Voldemort!

    a.   B'pashtus, we can answer that Hagrid was just being hyperbolic.

    b.   Or, perhaps, Hagrid deliberately refrained from mentioning Sirius because he did not want to get into a much longer discussion of Harry's parents' death.

V.   As Harry and Hagrid descend deeper and deeper into the tunnels of Gringotts, the air is described as getting continuously colder. Scientifically, once you reach the point of geothermal gradient, the temperature gets hotter the deeper you descend!

    a.   For whatever reasons, the Gringotts security staff obviously used magic to change the normal course of events with regard to temperature near the vaults.

VI.   Wizarding economics seems to make no sense. For example, an Ollivander wand, which contains an expensive core (unicorn hair, for example, valued at *ten* Galleons apiece) is priced at only *seven* Galleons. Furthermore, according to JKR, one galleon is equivalent to (approximately) five British pounds or seven American dollars — much, much less than its equivalent in gold. What stops wizards from melting down money and selling it as precious metals for a huge increase in price?

    a. It is possible that wands only contain part of the items used in their cores (e.g., half of a unicorn hair).

    b. Presumably, Gringotts coins are charmed to prevent them from being melted down or duplicated.

VII.   In Chapter Ten, when Professor Quirrell informs the Great Hall that there is a troll in the dungeons, Dumbledore orders all prefects to lead their Houses to their respective dormitories. What about the Slytherins — their dormitories are located in the dungeons!

    a. Dumbledore must have either forgotten this fact in the panic; or, he meant all Houses except for Slytherin.

Chamber of Secrets

I.   In Chapter Five, after being brutally beaten by the Whomping Willow, Arthur Weasley's Ford Anglia ejects Harry and Ron and their luggage before unaccountably becoming sentient and leaving. Ten chapters later, it mysteriously reappears to help Harry and Ron escape the clutches of Aragog.

    a. Deus ex machina, perhaps?

KASHRUS HAKISHUF

II.   Chapter Eight states that Nearly Headless Nick "took several deep breaths…" Since when do ghosts breathe?

      a. Perhaps it just means that Nick did the ghostly equivalent of human breathing.

III.   In Chapter Ten, during a Quidditch match, Harry is assaulted by the eponymous rogue Bludger. The entire Hogwarts, including teachers, is watching as Harry narrowly avoid being severely injured. Why doesn't anyone do anything?

      a. Apparently, violence is an accepted part of Quidditch, and the teachers take the Bludger in stride. V'domeh L'hockey.

IV.   The blind (no pun intended) luck of Basilisk's victims is patently ridiculous. Mrs. Norris happens to have a puddle in front of her; Colin Creevey happens to be looking through his camera; Justin Finch-Fletchley happens to be looking through Nearly Headless Nick, who is conveniently already dead… How can the Basilisk be so unlucky? And why didn't it eat any of the petrified victims?

      a. Hashgacha Pratis.

V.   Furthermore, how exactly did the Basilisk use the plumbing to travel across Hogwarts — the Basilisk is huge, while the plumbing system probably isn't!

      a. Kasha on a Ma'aseh.

48

VI.　When Harry and Ron finally discover the entrance
to the Chamber of Secrets, why on earth do they go
inside without contacting some teachers? Surely
they're not so stupid that they think they can defeat
a Basilisk by themselves?
    a.　As far as they knew (and they were, in fact,
correct), Ginny Weasley was in mortal
danger. It was Mamish Pikuach Nefesh;
there was no time to waste.

Prisoner of Azkaban
I.　At the beginning of Chapter Five, Harry, Ron, and
Hermione load their trunks and owls onto the
luggage rack of an empty compartment at the end of
the Hogwarts Express. Why, the, upon re-
embarking, do they need to search for a new
compartment? And how does their luggage
mysteriously wind up in the new compartment
together with Professor Lupin?
    a.　V'tzarich Lomar that it was actually the
same compartment, and Professor Lupin
somehow managed to enter that
compartment and fall asleep in the few
moments that Harry, Ron, and Hermione
had disembarked to say their goodbyes; the
book is just very ambiguous.

KASHRUS HAKISHUF

II. How do Azkaban escapees such as Sirius Black (and, later, Bellatrix Lestrange and Lucius Malfoy) get back their wands? Even if the wands were not destroyed, it would be quite difficult if not impossible for an escaped convict to locate them!
   a. V'tzarich Iyun.

III. Why didn't Fred and George Weasley, in possession of the Marauder's Map for several years, ever notice Peter Pettigrew on it?
   a. They either just didn't see him, or they chalked it up to a mistake, just as Harry originally does.

IV. Perhaps the biggest plothole in the entire series is the existence of time travel. Why can't any given character — Voldemort, for example — use a Time-Turner to rectify all of his mistakes?
   a. As Hermione explains to Harry, "awful things have happened when wizards have meddled with time…. Loads of them have ended up killing their past or future selves by mistake!" Evidently, wizards have tried to do so, with unpleasant results. There are obviously strict, binding regulations regarding how time travel can be used.

KASHRUS HAKISHUF

Goblet of Fire

I.   Chapter Two states that Harry "had only found out that Sirius was his godfather two months ago." In fact, Harry overheard that Sirius was his godfather on the Hogsmeade trip last December — eight months ago!

        a.   This must refer to Harry finding out that his godfather, Sirius, was innocent, which did occur two months previously. The Lashon is not so M'dakdeik.

II.   When the Weasleys pick up Harry from the Dursleys, they all return to the Burrow using only one pinch of Floo powder. Why then, in CS, does each individual need to use his own pinch of powder in order to travel?

        a.   Even though the book does not mention it, you have to be Medayeik that even here, each person used a new pinch of Floo powder.

III.   In that same chapter, Arthur Weasley uses magic several times, despite the strict laws against performing magic in the presence of Muggles. Why doesn't Harry receive a warning from the Ministry for this, as he does in CS and OP?

        a.   Mistamah Arthur Weasley, a Ministry employee, notified his superiors beforehand that he would most likely be doing so.

51

IV.   Regarding the Triwizard Tournament, although the first task takes place in the Quidditch arena, the following two — in the Lake and the maze — are hidden from sight of the spectators, meaning that the hundreds of students and teachers present spend (potentially) several hours watching absolutely nothing!

    a.   Mistamah there was some magical device used to show spectators exactly what was going on.

V.   The entire book revolves around the fact that the disguised Barty Crouch, Jr. somehow converted the Triwizard Cup into a Portkey so that Harry is transported to Voldemort upon touching it. Now, in order to touch the Cup, Harry needs to win it, so Crouch does extensive work to enable Harry to win it. Why didn't he simply turn any one of Harry's regular items into a Portkey much earlier in the year?

    a.   V'tzarich Iyun.

VI.   There are actually a lot of issues concerning that Portkey. Portkeys are set up to activate at a specific time, so how could the disguised Moody make the Cup transport Harry whenever he happened to touch it? Also, how is Harry able to use it to return from the graveyard to Hogwarts — Portkeys only work one way!

KASHRUS HAKISHUF

    a. It is quite possible that the disguised Crouch was in control of the Cup the entire time, turning it into a Portkey seconds before Harry touched it. And perhaps Voldemort once again used the Portus Charm, in the assumption that he would need it to travel to Hogwarts after killing Harry.

Order of the Phoenix

  I. In Chapter Three, when the advance guard comes to take Harry to Grimmauld Place, Harry is already in trouble for casting a Patronus Charm in the presence of a Muggle. Despite this, Tonks casts several spells (*Lumos*, *Scourgify* and *Locomotor Trunk*) and Moody casts a Disillusionment Charm on Harry while they are still at Privet Drive!

    a. It is possible that the Ministry only becomes informed of illegal magic used in the presence of Muggles.

  II. After introducing herself to Harry, Tonks tells him that she is an Auror and only qualified one year ago. But in Chapter Twenty-Nine, Professor McGonagall says, "I don't think anybody has been taken on in the last three years"!

    a. Apparently, Professor McGonagall forgot about Tonks.

KASHRUS HAKISHUF

III.   When Ron receives his prefect badge, Molly
       Weasley exclaims that everyone in the family has
       become a prefect. Surely Mrs. Weasley would not
       have forgotten that Charlie was a Quidditch captain,
       not a prefect!

   a.   This is a Ra'ayah that Charlie was also a
        prefect in addition to a Quidditch captain.

   b.   Perhaps Mrs. Weasley was simply equating
        the two, as Quidditch captains share status
        with prefects.

IV.   Right before that, in discussing the fates of former
      DADA teachers, Harry says, "One sacked, one
      dead, one's memory removed, and one locked in a
      trunk for nine months." The last three refer to
      Professors Quirrell, Lockhart, and Moody
      respectively, but who was sacked — Professor
      Lupin voluntarily resigned!

   a.   Harry must have considered Lupin's forced
        resignation due to Snape revealing that he
        was a werewolf as a sacking.

V.   Chapter Sixteen mentions that one of the students
      who comes to meet with Harry in the Hog's Head is
      Dennis Creevey. How could he have come —
      Dennis was only in his second year, and therefore
      not allowed to visit Hogsmeade!

   a.   The only possible explanation would appear
        to be that the Weasley twins, quite

irresponsibly (K'darkam Bakodesh), let him know about one of the secret passageways.

VI.   In Chapter Twenty-Nine, Professor McGonagall tells Harry that in order to become an Auror he will need a minimum of five N.E.W.T.s. She then goes on to list four subjects: Defense Against the Dark Arts, Transfiguration, Charms, and Potions. What happened to the fifth subject?

    a. As she was constantly being interrupted by Professor Umbridge, McGonagall may have simply forgotten to mention it.

Half-Blood Prince

I.   In Chapter Sixteen, upon examining the potions book of the Half-Blood Prince, Harry notes that it could not have belonged to his father, since its publication date was nearly five decades ago. How, then, could the book have belonged to Snape, who was in the same year as James Potter?

    a. Young Severus Snape must have bought an old edition of the potions book several years after it was first published.

II.   In Chapter Twenty-Three, while discussing potential Horcruxes, Dumbledore tells Harry that the only known relic of Godric Gryffindor is his sword. What about the Sorting Hat?

    a. Although the Sorting Hat did originally belong to Gryffindor, it was enchanted by all four of the Hogwarts founders, effectively making it Hogwarts property; so, strictly speaking, the hat did not belong to Gryffindor.

    b. Perhaps Dumbledore was ignoring the Sorting Hat since he (correctly) assumed that Voldemort would not deign to deposit a part of his soul in such a dilapidated and dirty inglorious relic.

III.   Right before the events that lead to Dumbledore's death, Dumbledore casts a body-binding spell on Harry to prevent him from interfering. How could the spell have affected Harry — he is within the protection of the Invisibility Cloak!

    a. Apparently, the Cloak only protects its wearer from necessarily harmful magic; since Dumbledore had righteous intentions, the Cloak allowed his spell to pass through it.

    b. Also, we know that many of the general rules regarding magic seem not to apply to Dumbledore, an extremely talented and gifted wizard. We find, for example, that he was able to defeat Grindelwald despite the latter bearing the Elder Wand.

KASHRUS HAKISHUF

Deathly Hallows

I.   We see throughout the series that wizards can create and possess magical portraits of the deceased. Why couldn't Dumbledore, shortly before his death, arrange for a portrait of himself to be given to Harry when he embarks on his mission to locate the Horcruxes?

    a. V'tzarich Iyun.

II.   One of the main issues facing Harry, Ron, and Hermione when they are on the run is the lack of food. Gamp's Law notwithstanding, why can't Hermione increase the amount of food they do obtain, or use a Summoning Charm to access faraway victuals?

    a. Even the most talented individuals are not infallible. Hermione can't be expected to think of everything.

III.   In escaping from Malfoy Manor, Harry conjures a powerful spell using three wands simultaneously. Why is this occurrence not utilized more often?

    a. It is logical to assume that for security purposes the Ministry regulates all wands and only allows for the purchase of one wand per wizard.

IV.   In Chapter Twenty-Six, when Harry, Ron, and Hermione break into the Lestranges' vault in Gringotts, Hermione performs a whispered

KASHRUS HAKISHUF

Levicorpus spell to elevate Harry so that he can reach the Horcrux without touching the other contents of the vault. Why does Hermione speak out loud — *Levicorpus* is most effective as a nonverbal spell!

    a. Ein Hachah Nami; Hermione only speaks aloud to alert Harry of her intentions.

General Issues

I. Why are there any poor wizards (such as the Weasleys) — it's simple enough to transfigure the cheapest of items into expensive articles or to constantly enlarge foodstuffs!

II. Why does Voldemort (or whatever manifestation he is taking on) always wait until precisely the end of the school year to stage his evil denouement?

III. While wizard students learn plenty of magic, Hogwarts does not teach any basic skills like reading, writing, or math. Why aren't all wizards completely ignorant?

IV. What are the Gedarim for determining who gets Sorted into Slytherin? Slytherin has an unfortunate reputation of catering to the desires of evil and often potentially Dark students. Does the Hat sort anyone with evil intentions into Slytherin, regardless of intelligence or ambition? If this is the case,

KASHRUS HAKISHUF

wouldn't it make sense to do away with Slytherin
House (and the blatant prejudice against it)
altogether?

PART FOUR: CHILUFEI GIRSA'OS V'SHINUY NUSCHA'OS

KASHRUS HAKISHUF

Book Chapter: Page	Original Version	Corrected Version
SS 1:16	"I'll be takin' Sirius his bike back."	"I'd best get this bike away."
SS 5:72	"Dragon liver, seventeen Sickles an ounce, they're mad...."	"Dragon liver, sixteen Sickles an ounce, they're mad...."
SS 6:96	Harry noticed a shiny silver badge on his chest with the letter *P* on it.	Harry noticed a red and gold badge on his chest with the letter *P* on it.
SS 7:123	"I haven't eaten in nearly four hundred years," said the ghost.	"I haven't eaten in nearly five hundred years," said the ghost.
SS 16:265	"...yeh get a lot o' funny folk in the Hog's Head — that's the pub down in the village."	"...yeh get a lot o' funny folk in the Hog's Head — that's one of the pubs down in the village."
SS 16:282	"Well, Harry, you take the place of that bishop, and Hermione, you go next to him instead of that castle."	"Well, Harry, you take the place of that bishop, and Hermione, you go there instead of that castle."
SS 16:283	"I take one step forward and she'll	"I make my move and she'll take me

	take me — that leaves you free to checkmate the king, Harry!"	— that leaves you free to checkmate the king, Harry!"
CS 7:115	"He was the *on'y* man for the job," said Hagrid, offering them a plate of treacle fudge...	"He was the *on'y* man for the job," said Hagrid, offering them a plate of treacle toffee...
CS 7:116	...Hagrid's treacle fudge had cemented his jaws together.	...Hagrid's treacle toffee had cemented his jaws together.
CS 9:157	"Get — away — from — there —" Perry said, striding toward them...	"Get — away — from — there —" Percy said, striding toward them...
CS 14:257	Madam Pomfrey was bending over a fifth-year girl with long, curly hair.	Madam Pomfrey was bending over a sixth-year girl with long, curly hair.
CS 16:297	And the witch who banished the Bandon Banshee had a harelip.	And the witch who banished the Bandon Banshee had a hairy chin.
CS 18:332-333	"because Lord Voldemort — who *is* the last remaining ancestor of Salazar Slytherin — can	"because Lord Voldemort — who *is* the last remaining descendant of Salazar Slytherin

	speak Parseltongue.	— can speak Parseltongue.
PA 3:41	…when the bus moved abruptly from Anglesea to Aberdeen.	…when the bus moved abruptly from Anglesey to Aberdeen.
PA 3:41	"Righto," said Stan, "'old tight, then..." BANG.	"Righto," said Stan, "'old tight, then..." BANG!
PA 3:44	Two members of the Accidental Magic Reversal Department were dispatched…	Two members of the Accidental Magic Reversal Squad were dispatched…
PA 4:57	"Those are my books for Arithmancy, Care of Magical Creatures, Divination, the Study of Ancient Runes, Muggle Studies—"	"Those are my books for Arithmancy, Care of Magical Creatures, Divination, Study of Ancient Runes, Muggle Studies—"
PA 21:408	They saw Lupin, Ron, and Pettigrew clambering awkwardly out of the hole in the roots. Then came Hermione... then the unconscious	They saw Lupin, Ron and Pettigrew clambering awkwardly out of the hole in the roots, followed by the unconscious Snape, drifting

	Snape, drifting weirdly upward. Next came Harry and Black.	weirdly upward. Next came Harry, Hermione and Black.
PA 22:428	It took a moment for Harry to realize what Dumblefore had said.	It took a moment for Harry to realize what Dumbledore had said.
GF 7:89	"Cheers," said George, taking the slip of parchment Bagman handed him and tucking it away into the front of his robes.	"Cheers," said George, taking the slip of parchment Bagman handed him and tucking it away carefully.
GF 11:162	…a number of Filibuster's Fabulous No-Heat, Wet-Start Fireworks went off unexpectedly…	…a number of Filibuster's Fabulous Wet-Start, No-Heat Fireworks went off unexpectedly…
GF 24:667	…the man… …a tall man with untidy hair… …face of his father… "Your mother's coming..." he said quietly. "She wants to see you..."	…the woman… …a young woman with long hair… …face of his mother… "Your father's coming..." she said quietly. "He wants to see you..."

	And she came...first her head, then her body...a young woman with long hair, the smoky, shadowy form of Lily Potter... ...like her husband. She walked... ...and she spoke...	And he came...first his head, then his body...tall and untidy-haired like Harry, the smoky, shadowy form of James Potter... ...like his wife. He walked... ...and he spoke...
OP 6:102	"but perhaps we ought to let Mad-Eye have a shifty at it before we let it out — knowing my mother...	"but perhaps we ought to let Mad-Eye have a shufti at it before we let it out — knowing my mother...
OP 10:196	...so he allowed himself to be shunted forward on to the dark rain-washed road outside Hogsmeade Station.	...so he allowed himself to be shunted forward on to the dark rain-washed road outside Hogsmeade station.
HBP 1:10	The site, therefore, of Fudge stepping out of the fire once more...	The sight, therefore, of Fudge stepping out of the fire once more...

HBP 5:103	"Yep — ten 'Outstandings' and one 'Exceeds Expectations' at Defense Against the Dark Arts."	"Yep — nine 'Outstandings' and one 'Exceeds Expectations' at Defense Against the Dark Arts."
HBP 13:269	...with nothing in it except an old wardrobe and an iron bedstead.	...with nothing in it except an old wardrobe, a wooden chair, and an iron bedstead.
HBP 16:342	...straightening her hat. Have a little purkey, or some tooding.	...straightening her hat. "Have a little purkey, or some tooding.
HBP 22:476	'Yeah, I s'pose I'd better,' said Harry. 'I don't reckon I'll need all of it, not twenty-four hours' worth, it can't take all night....	'Yeah, I s'pose I'd better,' said Harry. 'I don't reckon I'll need all of it, not twelve hours' worth, it can't take all night....
HBP 27:591-592	"He cannot kill you if you are already dead. Come over to the right side, Draco, and we can hide you more completely than you can possibly imagine. What is	"Come over to the right side, Draco, and we can hide you more completely than you can possibly imagine. What is more, I can send members of the Order to your

more, I can send members of the Order to your mother tonight to hide her likewise. Nobody would be surprised that you had died in your attempt to kill me — forgive me, but Lord Voldemort probably expects it. Nor would the Death Eaters be surprised that we had captured and killed your mother — it is what they would do themselves, after all. Your father is safe at the moment in Azkaban...when the time comes, we can protect him too. Come over to the right side, Draco...you are not a killer..."

mother tonight to hide her likewise. Your father is safe at the moment in Azkaban...when the time comes, we can protect him too...come over to the right side, Draco...you are not a killer..."

APPENDICES

KASHRUS HAKISHUF

Appendix A: Confessions

"As obsessive fans will tell you, I do slip up! Several classrooms move floors mysteriously between books and these are the least serious continuity errors! Most of the fansites will point you in the direction of my mistakes. But the essentials remain consistent from book to book because the story has been plotted for a long time and it is clear in my mind."

—J. K. Rowling, interview archived at:

http://web.archive.org/web/20110607110538/http://www.jkrowling.com/textonly/en/faq_view.cfm?id=108

"Maths is not my strong suit."

—J. K. Rowling, interview archived at:

http://www.jkrowling.com/textonly/en/faq_view.cfm?id=63

KASHRUS HAKISHUF

Appendix B: The Hogwarts School Song: A Free Translation into Yiddish

<u>די שולע ליד פון האגוואַרץ</u>

האָגוואַרץ, האָגוואַרץ, האָגגי וואָרטי האָגוואַרץ,

לערנען אונדז ביטע עפּעס,

צי מיר אַלט און ליסע זײַן,

אָדער יונג מיט פּאַרשיװע ניס,

אונדזער קאָפּ געקענט מיט פּילונג טאָן,

מיט עטלעכע טשיקאַװע שטאָפֿן,

פֿאַר איצט זײַ ניטאָ נאַקעט און פֿול פון לופֿט,

דעד פֿליעס און ביטן פּוך פון,

אַזוי לערנען אונדז זאַכן ווערט געװאָוסט,

ברענגען צוריק וואָס מיר וװע פֿאַרגעסן,

נאָר טאָן דײַן בעסטער, מיר וועט די רו טאָן,

און לערן ביז אונדזער סײַכל אַלע פֿוילן.

Appendix C: References to the Number Seven

The Harry Potter series contains an inordinate amount of references to the number seven. These include:

- There are seven years of studies at Hogwarts.
- Harry's birthday is in July, the seventh month of the year.
- The Weasley family has seven children.
- Dumbledore's office, Professor Flitwick's office, the Room of Requirement, and Gryffindor Tower are all located on the seventh floor of Hogwarts.
- There are seven Quidditch players on a team, and seven hundred ways to commit a foul in Quidditch.
- Gryffindor hadn't won the house cup for seven years before Harry came.
- Quidditch practice is held at seven o'clock in the evening.
- There are seven obstacles to obtaining the Sorcerer's Stone.
- Gilderoy Lockhart wrote seven books.
- There are seven hidden passageways out of Hogwarts shown on the Marauder's Map.
- There are seven Animagi registered with the Improper Use of Magic Office.
- The Triwizard Tournament was first established seven hundred years before its appearance in GF.

KASHRUS HAKISHUF

- Fred and George charge seven sickles for a canary cream.
- There are seven locks in Alastor Moody's trunk, and Moody is locked in the trunk's seventh compartment.
- Frank Bryce is said to be nearing his seventy-seventh birthday.
- After hearing a loud, cracking noise while watching the news, Uncle Vernon waves from the window at "Mrs. Number Seven, who was glaring from behind her net curtains."
- Clause Seven of the Decree for the Reasonable Restriction of Underage Sorcery states that magic may be used before Muggles in exceptional circumstances.
- The boggart in the desk at Grimmauld Place changes seven times to reflect Mrs. Weasley's worst fears.
- When Harry falls down the stairs into the room with the veil at the Ministry of Magic, seven people come to his aid.
- The Ministry of Magic sends out a purple leaflet with seven ways to protect the home and family against dark forces.
- Harry and Ron each receive seven O.W.L.s.
- Voldemort splits his soul into seven Horcruxes.

KASHRUS HAKISHUF

Funnily enough, the number seven also famously occupies a special position in Yiddishkeit. Just a few examples of this include: Shabbos; Shmittah; Yovel; Sefiras Ha'omer; Shevah Brachos; Shivah; Ushpizin; Shivas Haminim; Sefiros; Yisro's names and daughters; days of Pesach and Sukkos; branches of the Menorah; Shevah Mitzvos D'rabanan; Shevah Mitzvos B'nei Noach; levels of Shamayim; Zayin Am'min; Nevios....

Coincidence? You decide.

About the Author

S. Y. Zeitlin is the author of the book you are now reading. A lifelong resident, like Lemony Snicket, he now divides his time, and is currently at work. This is his magnum opus (it's not his debut novel, since it's not a novel). He may be emailed at his email address.

www.ingramcontent.com/pod-product-compliance
Lightning Source LLC
Chambersburg PA
CBHW020339290526
45785CB00005B/2101